DON'T DRAG
THE POOP

MICHAEL ALLEN COOPER

DON'T DRAG
THE POOP

Don't Drag the Poop
Copyright © 2015 by Michael Allen Cooper. All rights reserved.

No part of this publication may be reproduced, stored in a retrieval system or transmitted in any way by any means, electronic, mechanical, photocopy, recording or otherwise without the prior permission of the author except as provided by USA copyright law.

This book is designed to provide accurate and authoritative information with regard to the subject matter covered. This information is given with the understanding that neither the author nor Imperium Publishing, Inc. is engaged in rendering legal, professional advice. Since the details of your situation are fact dependent, you should additionally seek the services of a competent professional.

The opinions expressed by the author are not necessarily those of Imperium Publishing, Inc.

Published by Imperium Publishing, Inc.
1097 N. 400th Rd | Baldwin City, Kansas 66006 USA
www.imperiumpublishing.com

Cover design by Roland Caballero
Interior Design by Jake Muelle

Published in the United States of America

ISBN: 978-1-64318-024-3
Religion / Christian Live / General

Contents

Introduction 7
I Am My Own Uncle 11
Mom Leaves 13
Know This 15
Run over Me 17
Side Note 25
Back to the Story 27
God Knows What Is Coming Our Way 29
What's Your Theory? 41
The Vision 43
The Next Chapter of My Life 49
Parables Are Good Stories 55
Prison on Earth Has Windows 57
By the Way, Before I Go 63

Introduction

Wouldn't it be nice to have the right words to say at all the right times? To never misquote anyone or any fact at any time? Life on earth doesn't really offer us that luxury, but it does point to a little known fact along those lines that is worth looking at. I can't count the times that I have really stuck my foot in it and proven that I am inept in some people's eyes, including my own. The quieter I have become, the more I realize I didn't know as much as I thought I did. I've been called a know-it-all, a braggart, and a smart aleck. I have been called worse, but that's another story.

The little known fact that I refer to is in the Scriptures. To paraphrase it would suffice here and as we delve into my life story, you will see that it has probably happened to you also at some point. The Lord has said, "Don't worry what you will say when they put you in front of the authorities, for your Heavenly Father will give you the words to say." ("He will help you with your answer so that you will not be considered an idiot.") Now the disclaimer would read something like this, you have to actually *read* the words of the Lord in order to know them and speak the word of God so that you are not ashamed of your answers. Now these words are not for the faint of heart, and since they are living and real, they carry a lot of meaning and weight. Whoa now, you might not believe that, and so we might have to back up just a minute and see where we've been and where we're going.

Walk with me while I tell you the rest of the story.

To make a long story short…

I was pretty young when I was born in Rapid City, South Dakota, so I have trouble remembering everything for the first few years, but some folks who were there told me a lot of things, and they are probably telling me like it was. For instance, when the doctors gave me penicillin, they say I broke out in hives and had some other bad reactions like convulsions. So now the thought is that I am allergic to it. Okay, well, I don't dispute it, and I just tell the new doctors in my life that I am allergic to penicillin, and they ask me what happened to me when I took it, and I tell them the story, and that is that. They just believe it and accept it as truth. Amazing.

I tell my friends and coworkers about being older where I was born. You see, we had to do more in those days because there was more to be done. My grandparents endured the Great Depression and believed in working very hard for everything. If you were going to the garage, you took something with you, and when you come back, bring certain things back with you. Every trip had to count for something more than just the trip alone. My grandfather didn't believe in slacking or giving money to kids that wasn't earned. According to how much I carried, I figure I was about three and a half or so when I was born. I went to work that same week and started buying my own clothes the next month. Just kidding, and I want to make sure you know that. Even so, hard work is a way of life growing up in a house with people who have been through the Great Depression. I worked for pay at the very earliest age. Spotting the nails on the bottom sheet of the Sheetrock in a house for a penny each was pretty big money when you are four years old. It was for my father, Bob G. Cooper, who did drywall and paint work.

My second actual paying job was for my grandfather, David R. Cooper, and was fifty cents a day for carrying gas cans, greasing the machinery at lunch, and carrying planks for bridging for the twenty-ton dragline. I had to watch when he moved the machine and later even drive it ahead now and then. He had a lot of heavy equipment. It was very rewarding to help out on the equipment when I was six to twelve years old. I learned about engines and other components of heavy equipment plus their operation. However, it can be dangerous, and I was run over by a heavy homemade camper trailer when I was three. More about that later. Cave-ins are a major concern. I had to be dug out one time when a ditch collapsed on my legs. The blood flow stopped immediately, and it was very painful.

My third official employment was in the sixth grade for my uncle Joe Baumberger as a carpenter's helper. I kept the jobsite clean and gathered any materials that needed to be stacked or carried to the carpenters. There were dozens of houses in a row to maintain, and it kept a guy busy to keep up. That first Friday evening, I got a check with my name on it for thirty-six dollars. I was so proud of that check I took it home and sat down across the table from my grandfather and showed it to him. I told him that I would be working for Joe from that time on. He said that would be fine and that I would have to pay twenty-five dollars a month for rent and buy my own school clothes plus help with the groceries. I agreed, and a wonderful thing happened: I learned to love to work and take some pride in providing for myself and the family.

So many these days look for ways to circumvent that idea. Work is very rewarding for the inner man. We need to accomplish things of worth to justify our being. When society allows us to escape that, we cheat ourselves out of that sense of reward of completion and fulfillment. The Heavenly Father says, "Six days shalt thou work, and on the seventh day, you should rest," and "You should also worship the Lord your God, and worship Him alone."

I Am My Own Uncle

Backing up a little, my parents divorced when I was three years old, and my sister Mary Ann was just a one-year-old baby. My grandparents on my father's side were awarded custody of us children with the intent of adopting us. So my father became my adopted brother. My half brothers and half sisters became my nephews and nieces. My cousins also became nieces and nephews. My aunts and uncles were now my sisters and brothers. My, it sounds like I became my own uncle. My uncle Donnie is now my brother.

Mom Leaves

I recall at the age of three standing on the couch and crying while looking out the window one night as my mother got into a car with some people, and my father saying, "Quit crying, she won't be back." They had been yelling at each other, and I was afraid. Is that supposed to make me not cry anymore?

The next time I saw her, I was ten, and we lived in Gillette, Wyoming. She had a three-year-old boy with her. He was my half brother by another father. I remember thinking, *He looks a lot like me.*

The next time I saw her, I was eighteen, and she didn't know what happened to the other son, Brandy Lind. His father had taken him, and there was no longer any communication between them. I watched the phone book in every town I went to, to see if I could find Brandy and through the years, gathered information about him. Later in life (forty-four years later), I found him through a search on the Internet. I had written letters to Oprah and Maury and others with no success. Mine was just another of thousands of requests. They wished me luck.

My father had remarried a Northern Cheyenne woman, Josephine Spottedwolf, and I have six brothers and sisters from that marriage.

My grandparents were old by other kids' standards, but I look back now and realize they were what I needed in order to be who I am today. I still go to the nursing homes and share. God had a plan for my life, and it worked. I can communicate with the older generation more effectively than the youth.

Know This

You will notice that I speak of God as though *you* believe in him. I base that on information in the Holy Scripture that says, "I have placed it in man's heart to know there is a God." End quote. So naturally *I believe God* over what a man claims he does or doesn't believe. A person can deny with their mouth anything they want, but it doesn't change the facts. A deep knowing in us is certain that there is something out there, and it's big. We all know it for sure.

Run over Me

When I got a little older, I started remembering stuff, but I made bad decisions a lot. Like the time I was four, my grandfather came home from a couple of weeks on a road construction job, and I decided to ride the pipe that attached the homemade trailer to the dump truck. He didn't see me duck in between the two vehicles, and after about twenty or so feet, I got bounced off, dragged, and ran over by the large homemade utility trailer full of tools. It also had a bed and cooking area in it.

After I woke up, I thought I better get off the road so I didn't get run over again. I crawled to the side of the road and used an old mail box to stand up. I must have had blood coming down by then because my grandmother came out of the house, saw me, and started running toward me. I passed out and woke up a few days later with bandages on my head due to the tearing away of the scalp. For many years, I had dreams about the wheel coming up my leg, over my chest, and over my face.

It was during this healing process that I figured out things about good and bad hiding spots. My uncle Donnie, who was now my adopted brother (four years older), wanted to play with my new toy cork gun, and since they had just been invented about then, they were quite novel. I didn't think he should be trusted to handle such a precious firearm, so I ran out of the house and hid behind the door so that when he came out and kept going, I could run back into the house and lock him out. My plan backfired; the doorknob hit me in the sutured area of the head. Needless to say, I learn too late sometimes. I also have not been very careful to avoid injury. Some would say, "He's an accident waiting to happen." This proves to be true throughout my life.

It was just about this period of my life that my right leg was completely bent and wouldn't straighten out. My grandmother, Goldie M. Cooper (Baker), would push and pull on it many times a day and put hot towels on the knee joint, causing me to cry and complain. The doctors were saying that it was polio most likely and that I would never be able to walk again normally. They did, however, have some new medicine and would we be willing to try it? They were calling it a polio vaccine. So, yes, we would try that stuff. Well, my stubborn grandma wasn't having any of that "can't walk" business, so the pushing and pulling, hot towel treatment, cussing the situation, and telling me that

I was going to walk if it was the last thing I ever did went on daily. One day, I saw a runner run by the house in his fancy silk running outfit, and I remember saying to myself and whoever listens to a child's heart, "If I am ever able to walk again, I will be the greatest runner and athlete this world has ever seen." Some months went by and Grandma, with God's help, got my leg straightened out and got me walking just in time for kindergarten. I didn't make it to the "greatest" status, but I sure tried. If we give all we can, that truly is success. That in itself is winning. Giving up has no place and no future. Try, try again. Never quit. I get discouraged at times, but I don't like to quit.

We moved from Rapid City to Flint, Michigan, for the winter, and each night after school, my uncle Donnie and I would walk to the top of a long hill to sled down to the house. On this particular evening, Donnie said, "Hey, Mike, let my girlfriend ride your sled, and you can walk home."

I, of course, said, "No, you will have to ride double," which was common in those days, and the argument ensued. My lights went out all of a sudden, and I found out later that Donnie had hit me in the head with a brick and left me for dead. Grandma asked Donnie later where I was, and he told her he didn't know and that the last time he saw me was up on the hill. She drove up there and found a pool of blood and started asking the people on the block if they had seen anything. Some folks told her they saw an ambulance a while ago. I woke up in the hospital with her crying over me and another bandaged head. I was also realizing that my uncle Donnie didn't want me around. More about that later.

We moved to Gillette, Wyoming, just in time for me to start the first grade; it was a small community, but busy and due for an oil boom. Everybody talked about it and knew it was coming. There were about 2,500 people there then, and most of the streets were gravel.

The men in our family did construction in various forms from dirt work to painting and everything in between. My granddad did dirt work and had a road grader, ditching machine, backhoe, dragline, dump truck, loader, and other machines. My father had a paint and drywall company. My uncle Joe had a house building company and did it all, from the footings up. Many others in the family either worked for one of them or had a small company that catered to local builders. I worked with them and worked on equipment.

I also had a set of homemade drums in the garage and took guitar lessons starting in the second grade. By the sixth grade, my musical interest turned to the cornet; and by the eighth grade, it was on the keyboards. So I really did not get accomplished on any of them. I just had a basic knowledge of how to play them. I would write songs, and when I played them, they were important compositions at the time. I remember sitting on the piano bench as a young child and watching my grandfather play ragtime hits, vaudeville numbers, and hits from silent pictures of yesteryear. He also played violin. Later in life, I played for him as he sat and listened and watched. I also found out that his father and grandfather played music too, mostly violin, and that there was a gifting through the generations of firstborn male children. They were all firstborn male offspring, like me and my father and his father, and so on up on the line. So there were five generations that I know of that were in the same situation. Firstborn, male, and musically inclined.

I didn't find out about this until my twenties when the Lord started giving me songs and dealing with my life musically, and the other generational things that stood out in the Cooper line. My son, Christian Michael, is also in that lineage, and he has musical talent also. He was a firstborn son, and I knew from an early age that I would have a son first and then a daughter. There is a quote in the Scriptures about the firstborn male son that opens the womb being reserved unto the Lord. I can see this being a reality in my family.

I had an uncle named Albert Cooper, who constantly talked about the Lord and the Bible. He had been a preacher in his life. The things he said about the Bible and God took root in my spirit, and that seed would later come to fruit. He just wouldn't stop talking about Jesus and God.

I didn't connect that it was for me until I was twenty-one years old.

I had a sports career that started in the second grade. I remembered I made a vow that "if I am ever able to walk, I will be the greatest athlete." We had a basketball game during the half time of the varsity game in about 1960. I was the tallest kid out there and had to wear Uncle Jack's tennis shoes, which were twice too big. My grandmother stuffed socks into the toes to fill them up. Our team won the game two to nothing. I was the only one that made a basket, and that was after many attempts. The crowd laughed and cheered, and I am sure we were quite the spectacle. They didn't know how serious it was for me.

Sports became my passion, and the coaches were like surrogate fathers to me. They would take me under their wings in a special way and make sure I had shoes, gym shorts, and other things. Part of our problem was that we didn't have much money and couldn't afford the shoes and equipment. Coaches would come to our house every year and get the papers signed for me to play because my grandmother was quite against me playing any sports. I had had too many near-death experiences and crippling incidents for her to just let it go. It would take quite an effort on their part to explain the insurance (which they also paid) school policies, and so on. And the part about "they would make sure I didn't get hurt" was really a whopper. I got hurt a lot in sports and played with a lot of pain most of the years I played. I was taken to a chiropractor two or three times a week in high school. (He said one of my legs was shorter so it caused pain to run and jump.) I had Jacuzzi and rubdowns daily, sometimes twice a day during high school. I played hurt almost all the time. Our trainer, Barney Cosner, was a master at keeping me going from week to week. He also had many other injured athletes to work on. He was the one reason I was able to compete. It took all summer to heal up from three sports' worth of injuries.

Early in my sports life, I also played summer baseball and was home run king several times. My grandfather on my mother's side, Floyd Fitzgerald, had a baseball team in Rapid City, and I had a distant cousin who played pro baseball for San Francisco. In little league, I and another guy, John, scored runs at the prestigious Miles City invitational to win the championship game two to one. I stole home to tie the score, and I know that sounds impossible, but Coach Kinzer explained how to do it during a brief time-out while I was on third base. I had stolen second and third, but stealing home was not done. I had a pulled groin muscle to show for it. John was batted in for that hard-earned win. Our trophy sat in the Stockman's Bank window for years. I would go by there daily to look at it. I would invite any new kids in town to come with me and view it. We would retell the story each time about the day we beat them all in Miles City.

Side Note

That same year, one of my best friends was killed by a drunk driver. My great-grandfather died of cancer. The next year, my best friend's brother was killed on his motorcycle. My girlfriend was killed in a car accident.

These types of events make you wonder about the meaning of life. I blamed myself for their deaths, and maybe it was because they all knew me. I decided that I wouldn't have any close friends anymore. Sometimes we are at a place we don't want to be. We have no control over it, and it teaches us some things. We get something, and we think, "It's not what I thought it would be," or "I guess I didn't want that after all."

Also, conversely, sometimes we are at a place, but we didn't know we wanted that. We are not sure how we got there, and the next step looks clear to us. Yesterday we wouldn't have chosen that at all. Today we see it a little differently. I just didn't know I wanted certain things until I had them. Kinda like the song: we don't know what we got till it's gone. This type of thinking will get your attention and lead you to examine your intents and purposes. That is a good thing if it leads you to truth. Caesar said, "What is truth?" Was he really looking for truth? He was intrigued by Jesus, and he saw truth incarnate. But he didn't understand what was happening right in front of his own eyes. The mission of the Christ could not be canceled by him or anyone else on earth. God chose a certain time to put Himself through this life, ordained a plan, and carried it out flawlessly by divine design. We only understand it partially.

Back to the Story

Our bragging rights got even bigger as we got older. We had undefeated seasons in basketball and football and were state champions in track as well. I normally placed high or won the shot put. I had an unorthodox style in the high jump, and the officials would try to disqualify me since I couldn't do the barrel-role style of high jumping. I would be upside down and backward. I got discouraged and gave up the high jump. A few years later, a guy named Fosbury broke the world record with the same style. My coach came to me and apologized for not sticking up for my style.

Normally, I won the half-mile run. I was second in the half mile two years in a row at state. I tied the school record of my hero, Mike Hladky. Our two-mile relay team set a new school and state record. Our teams became quite well-known around the state as a team to be reckoned with. *Team* is the key word here, and it takes several to make a team. The determination, dedication, and hard work it takes to win are really worth it all. We were winners even though we lost a few games here and there. Winning was a way of life. We expected to win, and most of the time, we did.

I had a neck injury my junior year and was not allowed to play football that year. I was not happy about that.

We only lost four basketball games that year.

We won state in track. We had big attitudes and could seem to back it up on the field and in the gym.

God Knows What Is Coming Our Way

Four weeks before my senior year, I fell about ten feet and landed on my back on a concrete slab. It stopped my heart, and I wasn't breathing. Some folks call that being dead. Two weeks before that, my uncle Joe had gone to Rapid City and took a new class that was being offered called CPR. None of us had heard of it; he read about it in the newspaper. So that day turned out fairly good considering I died for a few seconds. He did CPR and mouth-to-mouth on me, thus reviving me long before an ambulance could get there. There wasn't any 911 or cell phones back then. I had a concussion, cracked tailbone, cracked wrist, dislocated shoulders, cracked heel cups, and was generally beat-up real bad.

Two weeks later, when we started football, I was at the school early to get my stuff and get suited up. It took two coaches and more than an hour to talk Grandma into allowing me to play that year. I had to wait an extra week to have contact and wear special pads, but I was there with all my hurts. Barney had his hands full that year. Coach Mark Higdon also kept me able by manipulating my upper spine area by picking me up from behind.

During our first game with Kelly Walsh of Casper, I sustained another concussion, and Steve Noecker, the other guard and linebacker, would tell me my assignments before each play. I only missed one of those blocking assignments, and our halfback, John Fitch, got creamed in the backfield. He still reminds me of it now and then.

When we walked into the locker room after the game, my memory came back like a light bulb coming on, and I could remember all the plays again. Now I just had a concussion one month before that due to that fall. I also had a concussion during my sophomore year playing basketball. I was upended while driving in for a layup. Things like that were not understood back then. But I knew if the coaches found out I was having amnesia, they would pull me out. Now that I look back, I think that was probably the fifth concussion in my life.

I can point to dozens of places in my life where I know that God prevented me from dying or being permanently affected and debilitated. I thought everyone had those kinds of near-death events. I realize now how accident-prone I was and how blessed and protected I have been. Also, the enemy of our souls would like to destroy us and anything that God has made. Thank God, he is limited and can't take our life.

During my freshmen year, when it seemed like everyone around me was dying, I got into the Morman Church and got baptized and confirmed because my father was already in it. I learned a lot about Joseph Smith, the history of the LDS, and about all the opinions of the present-day church. I drifted away from it and quit going that same year.

During the next few years, I developed a theory about how things *really* were, how life had come about, why we are the way we are, and so on. Plus I didn't want any real close friends because they might die from being close to me.

* * *

When I was about to be a junior in high school, my uncle Joe and my grandfather helped me with the trade-in and cosigning so that I could buy a brand new '69 Camaro off the showroom floor. What a day it was, driving a car like that around town. I didn't want to go home. It had four on the floor, a 350 engine, and bucket seats. I even put in an eight-track player. Cassettes weren't invented yet. I had all the Beatles, Guess Who, Neil Diamond, and many others. Plus KOMA on the AM radio each night, what more could a guy want? We didn't have FM radio in Gillette, so we didn't miss it.

I had a deal with my uncle Joe that I would work for him as much as possible, which wasn't much during sports, and in the summer in exchange for him paying my car payment and giving me twenty dollars a week for gas (thirteen cents a gallon). He financed my life for the next two years of high school. During the summer, I gave up baseball to work for him full time. This seems like it would be an easy choice, but if you are sports-minded and you live for sports, it is a very hard decision. The sacrifice of giving up a sport is quite traumatic.

I always had the intent of making sports my life someday. But I felt like sports were over for me after my senior year of high school. I had been all district, all conference, and all state in football, basketball, and track, so I felt like I had accomplished it all. I wanted to play basketball in college and pros but was told I was too short. I was only six feet two inches. I was offered more than a dozen scholarships from various schools ranging from Rocky Mountain College in Billings to Dartmouth and Rutgers. I turned them all down because they wanted me to play football and track both. My body had been through the mill by then. I decided not to pursue sports in college and just go to a good architectural school. Having been a carpenter for several years and being in drafting class for four years, it seemed like the reasonable choice.

Once again my uncle Joe stepped up to help me. He paid the five-hundred-dollar earnest money fee to secure my spot into a prestigious school. Western Technical College in Denver was number five in the nation, so I went to Denver in the fall of 1970. I had a new Honda 450, and before they left Denver, my grandparents bought me a 1960 Pontiac Bonneville (convertible) so that I had a car. I was without my Camaro due to the drunken 85 mph T-bone wreck I had in the spring of '70. That is what drinking and driving will get you. There are some things in life that you really love, yet you never realize how much until they are gone. I know that is an overused cliché, but each person feels it differently at different times and ways so that it affects each life in that particular way to help them at that time. No two are the same in every way. All things are for our good if we love the LORD since we are called according to His purposes. I didn't love the LORD during that time of my life. He knew that I would later, so He was watching over me. I learned later in life that my will is not what is being imposed upon this universe. I was selfish, hot-tempered, and had a very high opinion of myself.

After a month at WTC, I overheard another guy talking about their basketball team having practice that night. I asked about it, and he said they were all set already due to last year's recruiting. I wouldn't quit though and went there that night to watch and, in the back of my mind, to try out. I asked the coach if I could try out, and he asked where I was from. I told him Gillette, Wyoming. He rolled his eyes, hemmed and hawed, but after a while, he finally realized I had my stuff there and was persistent. He allowed me to play with them that night, and I played every game that year as a forward.

I averaged twenty-seven points a game and a dozen rebounds. Our team got second in the regional tournament. I got a broken nose in the first half of that game, so my second half wasn't so good. After that championship game, I was stopped by a guy at my car while leaving. He gave me his card and introduced himself as a scout for the newly forming Denver Nuggets team. He asked if I would come and try out that summer. My dream of pro basketball was going to come true. But I never made it to that try out. I still had no idea that God was watching over me.

Life takes some turns that we don't expect, and the consequences can be quite harsh and eye-opening. We can live to regret some of our choices and then also realize that we had to go through certain things in order to fulfill our destiny. I would not be who I am today without making some of the wrong choices I have made. I am not proud of some of my past, but I can look in the mirror today without hate for that man in there, and I don't blame anyone but myself for my failures. I do not dwell on them, nor do I extol them to anyone. I know a lot about what not to do. My war stories are short and sweet or nonexistent. They are both common and rare due to the little details here and there. Just because something happened to us, we think we are unique. The results and future outcome is much more important. The eternal placement of our inner soul is critical for us, and the Father in heaven has only good and high hopes for us. Where will you be in ten thousand years? These types of questions came to me here and there, and I have to give an answer. We all do. Do I really care about things? Will I take some time to think about my eternal future? Will I reason it out and deal with my failure in the flesh? Will I consider my ways? How do I treat my fellow man? Is karma real, or is there more? This list could go on for hundreds of pages. We must ask the mundane and ridiculous questions as well as the deep and probing ones to be complete in life. Since we use a small portion of our brain, let's use it as wisely as possible. They say we use about 7 percent, some maybe less, some more. Either way, it's not much. We are not exactly superintelligent compared to the God who made this universe. He's the greatest scientist ever, and beyond that, He's also the top physicist in the known universe. We haven't invented anything. He already knew it all from the start. He is my source. I want only what

He gives, nothing more and nothing less. Since He knows all the facts, I can trust Him.

After college basketball in the spring of 1971, I worked at the Radisson Hotel / Playboy Club parking cars and planned on staying in Denver. I drove all kinds of cool cars. Tips were good, and the people I worked with were awesome. I called home to see how things were going, and my grandmother was crying because my grandfather was having another stroke. He had one during my senior year, and it was hard to watch the crippling effects of what a stroke does. He would be disabled for a while, and if they didn't fulfill the contract on the landfill dump, they would lose their house and everything they owned. She asked if I would help. I wanted to stay in Denver for that tryout. She pleaded with me. I said I would come back and help them. I never told her about the tryout. I felt as though I owed something to these folks who raised me without selfish regard to their own needs. They took me in because they wanted me, not because they had to. She must have loved me because she would whip me as a child for getting hurt as soon as she knew I was going to live through it. Getting spanked made us smarter.

I also didn't tell her that I had started smoking pot and snorting a little speed here and there. I kept it hidden pretty well for a while. My usage increased very rapidly due to an addictive personality. My hair was getting pretty long for Gillette standards. Some people noticed. It's hard to hide. Pot was getting popular about then, and even the high school kids in Gillette were trying it too. My friends all had long hair and taught me how to smoke cigarettes to enhance and prolong the high from the pot. Day after day, I operated the dozer at the landfill, and night after night, I chased those highs that were so hard to maintain. I had no focus or goal, I obviously didn't make it to the tryout camp for the Nuggets, so there was no reason anymore not to do drugs. I would work hard on the weekdays and party harder on the weekend.

My grandfather got better and returned to his Caterpillar operation at the landfill. I started working in the oilfields where there were lots of pot smokers, and I blended right in. Another new friend, T. R. Croy, introduced me to other drugs like LSD and heroin. We would help drill a hole or two and then drive to Boulder and score drugs of all kinds to resell, tryout, and get ours for free. Our lives were chaotic, and we thought that was okay. I overdosed a couple times and almost died, but that doesn't sway us if we're not done yet. We keep trying to find a way to maintain the drugged lifestyle. Once you are in the downward spiral of drugged-up death, it's hard to see clearly. You think you know what's best for you. It's a lie. You are in a rut and can't see out of it. I even moved out to Tacoma for a while to try to change. That didn't work. My uncle Joe would say,

"If you can't figure it out, figure out a way to figure it out." That has stayed with me all these years. I figure out ways to figure stuff out. I wasn't ready to figure out how to stay clean. I liked the highs and endured the lows as though they are just part of it.

I met a girl who changed my life. I moved back to Gillette from Tacoma to be near her. She was more than I had ever dreamed of, but the only problem was her mom. Her mom would always start talking about Jesus and His love. Man, she wouldn't stop. I had told her several times I didn't want to hear it. I would say, "Keep that crap to yourself." But she would eventually pull the conversation back in the direction of Jesus. It would get me mad real quick.

I had this theory going about a revolving chain-of-life universe, and it was my only truth about how things really got this way. I had become atheistic and agnostic. The only way the ancestors could stop the boys from killing each other and make them stop raping the girls was to tell them this story of the big chewy in the sky that would kill them if they didn't quit it. I was sure that the Bible was strictly just a well-developed made-up story and held no real answers. Part of that came from the fact that most of the people who talked about it did not have a changed life, nor did they abstain from anything that I was doing either. The so-called Christians were just like me, but really and truly deceived, or so I thought. I knew what was really going on. In my mind, I had the answer. Things just happened to evolve and recreate time after time through a series of life-chain cycles that were linked to each other and nothing else. Seemed simple and even some of the mystics kinda knew a little about it. The Beatles were trying to find it. I was one of the few that understood it now, so I was okay.

What's Your Theory?

I do remember one part of my theory that was a little troubling. I could rub two pieces of rock together and grind them into dust, but they would still be here in some form forever, and I wouldn't. I thought that was unfair and rather cruel. I only had a few moments on the eternal clock. Well, better party and enjoy them totally. Sleep the least amount possible, and do the most that I can do. It's the battle of evermore. It's the age-old question-and-answer session that has always been going on. What's real, and what isn't?

My girlfriend broke the news that she was pregnant. Well, it's the modern age; we could take care of that pretty easy. A couple of phone calls and a trip to Seattle where it was legal to abort these types of things seemed like the only solution. We drove to Washington where my mother lived, paid the small fee, and all was well. Right? Well, almost. There was a lot of pain involved with abortion. Physical, emotional, and spiritual. It can take a lifetime to get over it all. Sometimes we never recover totally. I can't imagine what the woman really feels permanently.

While in the Seattle area, I met and befriended some organized friends that offered me a position with them. I wanted to be included in what seemed to be important events. I wanted to be rich and powerful like them. Was this my future?

The tension kept growing by the hour. My girlfriend's anxiety kept growing, and I could tell she was getting uneasy about it. The man kept saying things like, "It's forever." The word *forever* can get your attention even if you don't believe in it. I even said that it's forever for *this life*, and he would say, "No, forever."

Well, now it was getting even tougher to see clearly on how to proceed.

The man then said, "Take a few days to think about it and call me." That sounded like a good idea, so I headed back to Wyoming. We stopped in Utah and Colorado to visit some old friends. It was going well for the next few days until one night, while sitting in my friend's living room and watching a movie, the room went totally black. Eyes open or closed, it didn't matter. The darkest black I had ever seen was now all around me.

The Vision

There was no longer any sound, light, or presence of any other people. I knew I was blinking hard and straining to see and move, but there was nothingness all around me. Everything was blacker than I had ever seen before, and all things were gone. *All things*. The torment down inside started very quickly. Anguish, regret, torment, and lonesomeness like I had never felt were the only things I could really feel right then. Agonizing. Separation from all things.

During this moment, a voice started speaking to me. I didn't recognize the voice, and it was not my inner voice. He said, "You have been offered this lifestyle, the end result is blackness, torment, and outer darkness for eternity." Now this torment was intense, real, and growing steadily worse. Needless to say, I didn't like it.

Then the inflection of the voice changed while the darkness faded, and the place I was at grew into light, warmth, and comfort. The light in fact became brighter than the sunlight. Yet it did not hurt my eyes, and it was a liquid living light that flowed into me and out of me with my breath and in and out of my skin and bones too. I would open and close my eyes but the light was ever present like I had no eyelids. Eyes opened or closed, it didn't matter, the comfort, peace, and serenity felt in this place had no words in our language to express it. It was the realest of anything that I had ever felt in my entire life. The voice was more inviting and pleasant when he continued. He said, "But I can give you eternal life, peace, joy, and the things that you really desire in your heart. Now you have to make a choice."

While he was talking, this time, I knew beyond the shadow of any doubt that this was Jesus, the Son of God, and that He was the all-powerful and eternal Supreme Being all in one. There was absolutely no doubt who this was speaking to me. As He faded away from my inner being, I found myself in the living room again, and the movie on TV was still playing. The other people, including my girlfriend, were still sitting there watching and had heard nothing, seen nothing, and knew nothing about what had just happened to me. I immediately excused myself from the room and went to the bedroom. After a few minutes, my girlfriend came into the room and found me lying there quietly. I was in awe at what had just happened.

She said, "What's wrong?"

I asked her if she believed in God.

"Yes", she replied.

I asked her if she also believed in Jesus.

"Yes."

"Do you believe there's a heaven and a hell?"

"Yes. What's going on?"

"Do you believe there's a devil and all that?"

"Yes. What's going on?"

I asked her why she hadn't said anything about it to me.

"You didn't want to hear it."

She was right. I hadn't wanted to hear it. In fact I had been adamant about it. I said, "Well, how do you know about all this?"

She then explained her life to me and shared how she had been raised in church and had it forced on her all her life and that she had rebelled against it. Her father was a preacher for a while; he had preached it to her, but she was living in doubt and in sinful backsliding conditions. We met during this time, and she had been wanting to get back to the church life and especially wanted away from me if I chose the life with organized crime. "What's going on?" She persisted to know.

I finally told her that Jesus had just spoken to me out in the other room. She cried and explained that I was sitting wide-eyed back at the living room. She had called her mother days before and asked for prayer.

All of a sudden I was okay with that. I wasn't mad at her for asking for prayer, and in fact, I was thankful. Now

I knew for sure that Jesus did exist. I remember thinking, *Everything is going to be okay. He will make all things right in the end.* I went to sleep peacefully, something I had never known before. Just the fact that Jesus is real changed everything.

The next morning I showered and found myself singing a Billy Preston song that I had heard. "That's the way God planned it. That's the way God wants it to be."

Later while driving to the store, I was asking down deep if that really happened last night or if I was just having the effects of some previous drugs. Finally, I said out loud into the car, "Are you really real?"

Then his voice spoke into my car out loud, "Yes!" Quietly He added, "I am with you always."

At that point, I broke down and repented of all my past sins and evil nature. The Lord must have had some angels on standby to steer the car while I wept and cried to the God that I had just met. I was cleansed, redeemed, and restarted in that moment. I was forgiven forever.

The drive back to Wyoming included a guy who needed a ride to Laramie. The car was quiet for a long time, and he finally said, "So, Mike, what are you going to do when you get back to Gillette?"

Without hesitation, I said, "I am going to get me a Bible and study it and tell everybody in the whole wide world about Jesus."

His jaw dropped to his chest, and I had my first witnessing session. This was from one long-haired hippy to another. I told him about the night before and that he was in the room while it happened. I told him about the taste of hell and of heaven that I had seen and felt and that Jesus was real and alive. My passion was already growing, and I was more than sure about that part of what I knew to be real: Jesus is alive.

We dropped him off in Laramie, and the drive to Gillette went quickly. We discussed the whole vision in detail many times. I told my girlfriend not to say anything to her parents or anyone about this event that had changed my life. I was thinking that I should be the one to tell any and all about Jesus speaking to me. Her folks lived about twenty miles south of town, and we stopped to visit. It was a big house, and the dining area sat all nine of them and then some. Seven kids, the parents, and me. They were visiting along, and the dad asked, "Well, what's new with you, Mike?"

Well, I barely got the words, "Jesus spoke to me last night," out of my mouth when he almost hit the ceiling with his hands up and yelling, "Praise God!" and "Thank you, Lord!" and "Hallelujah!" and stuff like that. He was running around the dining table and kept shaking my hand. Scared me a bit, and made me think he might be kinda crazy.

Her mom was weeping by then and hugging us and making me very uncomfortable. All the other brothers and sisters were running through the house and yelling things like "Praise the Lord!" I wanted out of that house right then. This family was definitely insane. I left the girlfriend there too.

Now it's one thing to tell believers about this type of experience; it's quite another to tell my own family who mostly don't have a clue about God. I knew there would be a lot of different reactions.

Uncle Albert used to talk about Jesus and God, but everyone would leave the room, and some would even tell him to keep it to himself and be rude to him. Some of them would not believe I had changed. I had destroyed the trust and relationship with many in my family.

After telling Uncle Jack Cooper, he said he had heard my name on the radio last week. He said he was out deer hunting one Sunday morning and C. M. Ward the revival time speaker in Springfield, Missouri, mentioned that a sister from Gillette, Wyoming, had requested prayer for her daughter who was dating a drug dealer named Mike Cooper. He asked that people pray for her daughter and her drug dealer boyfriend, Mike Cooper. I thought, *Oh no, now everybody will know what I have been doing.* They knew already. People across this country had been praying for my salvation. I didn't stand a chance. Thanks be to God. Prayer changes things.

The Next Chapter of My Life

That week I saw my girlfriend's dad. He asked if I would be going to church. I told him I would be going to the Morman Church since I was baptized and confirmed there. He said, "Oh, well, I sure would like you to visit our church, the Assembly of God."

I said I would sometime. I read the Bible incessantly. During breaks at work, morning and night. I couldn't get enough of what Jesus had to say.

I walked into the LDS church that Sunday with Jesus in my heart and sat quietly while everyone testified about Joseph Smith and his astonishing feats. I was finally asked if I had any testimony. I told them about Jesus and His love and how He had spoken to me and that Joseph Smith was probably just another guy like us who was hungry for the LORD. Then I was taken by the arms and led to the backdoor and escorted to my car. I was told that I can't speak against Joseph Smith like that, and if I persisted, I would be banned from the church. I tried to explain that I just wanted to help them find Jesus. I was also told if I continued like this, my name would be removed from the cave. I told them that Jesus would not be stopping by the cave to see *their* book of life. He had his own, and He had it memorized. Needless to say, I was not feeling welcome there anymore.

The next Sunday I tried out the first Assemblies of God church. Orvil Holden became my mentor and asked me extensively about my conversion. They clapped and hollered, "Hallelujah" and "praise God" when I shared the vision of hell and heaven and the part about Jesus speaking to me was welcomed with hands held high, weeping, and singing and rejoicing. When the altar call came at the end of the service, I almost ran to the altar.

I couldn't get enough of hearing about Jesus. The next spring I was asked to play the role of Jesus in our church play for Easter. I still had long hair and a beard, so I didn't need much makeup. What an anointed night that was.

Playing the part of Jesus gave me a new inner fire for the things of the Lord. It was a reenactment of the judgment seat of Christ. We will face Him someday, without a doubt, either as a friend or a foe. It's our choice. He made His choice very clear. We should too. There is no neutral ground, even though there seems to be a lot of those who wish there was. He asks us to trust and believe by faith.

Walk with Him and talk with Him. That takes time. Once we run out of time, it's too late; it's the finish line. My best advice to anyone whether they are interested in Him or not is to find out before you get to the finish line. It takes desire. It takes practice. Hard work. Time. Patience. Love. Perseverance. These things I learned in sports, at practice, and in the games. The coaches, players, and the rules of the game allowed me to see what it takes and how to attain it. It's not easy, and neither is anything worth having. Disqualification is a real hard lesson. The oldest trick in the book is to distract us from our real goal. If we are willing to give it our all, then we can be a winner. A long time ago God sent his Son to bring us the Word of His plan. If we read, contemplate, and do the Word, we win. Winning is everything in this case because we can't afford to lose our immortal soul to an outer darkness that has nothing at all to offer, especially due to a hasty or impetuous decision on our part and we don't have all the facts. Totally alone and tormented in the knowledge that we could have changed if we just tried. I heard so many say, "All my friends will be there." That's a lie. Each one will think they are the only one there. There's no interaction or love. Uncle Albert used to say it was like searching for the handrail to a stairway in the dark. Groping around forever. I will examine things now, rather than take the chance of losing the most important race I ever ran. Will you consider your ways?

Rejecting the Creator and His plan is to say you don't want what He created either. Many would say at this point,

"God wouldn't do that," but His word says He will, and we know that He has never lied. He commended His love toward us in that "while we were yet sinners, He died for us." What more would you have Him do? Our adversary lies and is the father of all lies. He wants to take as many with him to hell as possible. He hates God and all God stands for. So I presume if you are still reading this, you do not hate God and all that He stands for. If you *do* hate the LORD, then you already know you have no hope in your future. It will end someday with separation from God and all His creation.

You say He would not be fair in doing that. He says, "It is the only fair way to do it." So who do you believe? There will never be another rebellion in the New Jerusalem, and there is no one there who can't be trusted. Can you be trusted? God knew all things before time began, so He paid the ultimate price to redeem those who would choose Him. Not from fear or with ulterior motives. But from the basis of love. There will never be a time in eternity that someone says, "Hey, let's try this," and goes off in an evil direction with one third of heaven following. That just won't happen again. It won't even be considered because we will know what the outcome of that is beforehand. If the race has an oval track, but we continually run straight, then we get off course and lose sight of the finish line and obvious victory. Same thing if the race has a straight course profile forever, we can't start running circles. We know it would lead us to the wrong place. Don't be disqualified due to stubbornness.

The word *choice* says more than we can fathom. We choose many things to complete our life, and then we have consequences to go with our choices. I could stop right there and leave you to make your choice. Do you have all the facts? Do you know enough to make an eternal decision? Would it be fair and logical? Make it a wise one and stay with it. Or I could continue to tell you a few more things that brought me to my choice. We all have a deep desire in us that only God himself can fill. It is like a vacuum, and only He can fill it. No drug, booze, or manufactured thing will do. We try it all, but nothing satisfies. We ache for the realness and closeness of God. He created that inner void, and He alone can fill it.

If you are still reading this, I can presume you don't hate God, and you might even want to walk with Him. Cool. Don't be angry at Him either since you don't have all the facts; you can't make a fair judgment. Only He has all the facts. I can tell you that if you choose Him, He will never leave you nor forsake you. He will eventually make all things clear to you. He cares for you so much that He died for you. Most people wouldn't die for anything or anybody. There are some who would die for a good cause or good people.

Jesus is God incarnate. Pharaoh was not God incarnate. Jesus is. God is not Ra or Allah or any other named god.

He never has gone by those names. He proved it in many ways. Many times over and over. He spoke about it and then rose Himself from the dead to prove it. No other name can compare with His. This plan was created by God himself to separate all the believers from the nonbelievers. The foolishness of the Lord is wiser than all our wisdom. We can't see yet why this was the best plan, and God asks us to accept it by faith and believe it and act upon it. Someday we will say, "Oh now I see it all, and it's good."

Such a simple plan, yet so complex. To use the rebellious one to prove the faithful one. Allow the weeds to grow along with the grain side by side. The separation will come at the last trumpet. All the dead will be brought alive into His presence. Every knee will bow to Him and proclaim, "Jesus is Lord."

Parables Are Good Stories

He built a vineyard (earth) and leased it out to vine dressers (us). He then went away on a long journey, and when He comes back, what will He find? Faith? Unbelief? Hate? Disgust? Love? What will He find in you? That is the question.

Choose this day whom you will believe, serve, and love. Before it's too late. Practice at it. Get good at it. Don't deceive. Remember, if God can't trust us, we won't be there. Be real and honest with God. He already knows all our faults and shortcomings anyway, so admit them freely to him. In fact He says that if we confess our sins to Him, He is faithful and just to forgive us for them. Talk to Him. Prayer is talking with the Almighty God. Bare your soul to Him. Plead your case to Him. God is Jehovah, and He is the only one and true God. He is the God of Abraham, Isaac, and Jacob. He is the God of the living. Are you living? You can be more alive than ever before. We die daily, so He can live in us.

* * *

I married my girlfriend, and we had two wonderful children. Years later, I ruined that marriage by being a cheat. When our marriage fell apart due to my infidelity, I blamed God for the inability to hold us together. I expected a miraculous thing to happen no matter what, and when it didn't, I became angry and resentful. I basically told Him to leave me alone, so He did.

I chose to run around with the type of people I had known back in the drug-filled days, and it wasn't long before I was using drugs again. I relapsed, or backslid as the Christians say. I had eight or so years of clean time and had gotten to know Jesus. However, I was mad at Him and went my own way. I cried myself to sleep nightly for many years. I was hooked on cocaine and going off the deep end fast. I tried to overdose myself to end the madness. I remember the disgust when I woke up to see that I was still alive. The next morning at four o'clock, the DEA broke in my door and arrested me for sales of a controlled substance. I spent some time in county jail and was still mad at God. I still cried myself to sleep most nights. I was in and out of jail due to revocations.

Prison on Earth Has Windows

I was in the fish tank in the Wyoming State Pen after being processed into the penitentiary. It would be thirty days before I go to population. I was sleeping on the floor on a thin mattress each night due to overcrowding. I shared a cell for a few days with a guy who was almost done with his thirty-day wait. Daily, we got one hour out of the cell for showers, walking, reading, and so on. During this other guy's hour, he would come and tell my cellie about the Lord. I acted like I couldn't hear them. I thought I knew more about that subject than him anyway. Finally my cellie got out, and I had the cell to myself. I was thinking the Jesus preacher would quit coming by now that his friend was gone. Wrong. He came the next day. I told him his friend was gone and I didn't want to hear about Jesus, thanks anyway. He wouldn't take no for an answer and asked my name. I didn't want to tell him. I knew what he was up to; he was trying to witness.

"Mike Cooper," I said.

"My sister used to date a guy named Mike Cooper up in Gillette."

"Are you kidding me?" I said. "What's her name?"

"Cindy."

Well, it turned out that her little brother Billy had been in prison for many years, and here he was, wanting to tell me about Jesus. I realized there was no escape from the presence of God. He wanted me back. Billy had gotten saved while in prison, and now he helped me give my life back to Jesus. I repented again. The place began to shake, and I thought the walls were going to fall down.

I said to the Lord, "What's going on?"

He said, "That's the devil, and he's mad that you have come back to me because he knows you are going to reach many for me. When you get into population, get a guitar and sing your songs in the chapel for the prisoners."

"But, Lord, I can't remember them and my sheets of music are in Gillette."

"I gave them to you once. I can do it again."

He also added that those songs would be heard in the deepest, darkest prisons in Africa someday. I wondered at that, but I didn't doubt it, for I know He keeps His word and fulfills it. The next day, the newspaper said there was a 5.7 earthquake with an epicenter close to the penitentiary. It seemed like a coincidence to humans, but I know what God said. I believe *Him*.

I rented a guitar from another inmate, and he waived the fee when he heard why I needed it. I sang songs in the chapel, shared my testimony, and started a daily devotional meeting at noon right after lunch. We only had three men the first day. In a week, we had about a dozen, and it was growing steadily. Men would walk by close enough to hear us, and some would stop and join in.

Now when I first got to Rawlins, I had written a short three-sentence letter to the district judge, stating that I didn't belong in that place and asking that he reconsider. I had forgotten about that letter and was busy doing what I thought would be my prison ministry. After about three months, they took me to Gillette for a sentence reduction hearing. The judge stated that he had also gotten a letter of good things that I had done there from the warden and my case worker, like teaching carpentry, leading worship in chapel, playing on the prison basketball team downtown, working on the old territorial prison with a minimum security team. He was impressed, I could tell. He sternly warned me as he let me go that if I screw up again, I would do all my two- to five-year sentence. I know he meant it, but I knew I would be okay now that I was free and recommitted to the Lord again. I had several more years of probation to serve and a five-thousand-dollar fine to pay.

Shortly after that, I married my new best friend, Gail, on August 5, 1985. She was from Sheridan, Wyoming. Later we made our home in Sheridan. I have lived here since 1986. We raised three boys there and still live there today.

I spent seven years working in the recovery field helping addicts and alcoholics. I would tell them about my life while on drugs and since my conversion. I also told them, "Don't drag the poop. Let it go." Don't bring that bag of poop into the future and expect others to look at it and examine it with you. We all have a bag of it, and we can let it go. Other than the brief stints of recovery work, coal mine, and in the oilfields, I have been in construction almost entirely. I have had several surgeries for various reasons: back surgery, knee replacement, five rotator cuff repairs, left hand, both elbows, and so on, and the old body is getting tired. But I have the Lord, love, grace, and mercy in my life. I couldn't have imagined nor designed a better way to come to terms with the eternal God. He only wants good things for us, and if we allow it, He will give us the kind of peace that is unknown in this world. Peace that surpasses all understanding.

I played music at the nursing homes, churches, and wherever I was invited for the last several years. Sometimes it's in a private home for the sick and dying. I played a set in Romania during a mission trip in 2010. I have waited for God to direct the path for the music to grow and travel to Africa. I was able to make a CD with Tate Music Group lately. One copy of the CD went to Cameroon, Africa, with Bishop James. Only God knows how He will use it. I hope to make more CDs of songs that God shares with me. I help with sound and computer and sing backup at our local church. Occasionally, I lead worship on a Wednesday evening. I still play monthly at the nursing home. I have hoped to write the story of my life since 1972 when I first found out that Jesus was real, but many things had to happen first. Who could have known what was in store?

The future looks bright, and I will sing to and about Jesus every chance I get. I tell as many people as I can that Jesus is alive. I hope to see you in the future realm that has no bounds or limits. Nothing I say or do can convince anyone to believe, but if you choose to investigate it a little more due to something I said, then this work has been successful. May the purity, fairness, and love of the Ancient of Days be with you and clothe you forever and ever. Be blessed. Rest and be refreshed in Jesus. No greater love has any man than to lay down his life for his fellow man.

PS. I hope to hear your life story someday. If you have any questions or comments about my life story, please feel free to contact me on Facebook.

By the Way, Before I Go

We hear all the usual sayings: Just do it. You never know 'til you try. If it feels good, do it. I'll try anything once. It won't kill you to try it. Go for it.

Then there's "holy cow" (Is this based on the golden calf the Israelites made?) and "holy mackerel" (Is this based on the tax money that Peter found in the fishes mouth?).

Other thoughts and ideas: God says He had no beginning, so is the clock we have on our wall the correct time?

How does the timing of the rebellion of Satan line up with the creation? Before or after it?

Before Noah's flood, the sons of God (Satan and his henchmen) were having relations with human women and producing giants and men of renown that created the old stories of Greek mythology. Is that why the flood had to come and start all over? So that humanity had a fair chance to make the kind of decisions we need to make? Only Noah and his wife, his sons, and their wives survived. Before the flood, people live many hundreds of years. After the flood, one hundred twenty or less.

Whether an angel did or didn't have any part of the rebellion surely cast some doubts in the heavenly realm. Did some of them quickly volunteer to go to earth as a baby and be born and live to show their loyalty? Did that show what their choice would be forever? God says He knew us before He formed us in the womb. He also says He gives the spirit to a person. Wouldn't that be a way to see what a spirit would do given the multitude of temptations we face on earth? How long would it take to put all the angels through the proving grounds called earth? And if God wanted as many as possible with Him forever, then it might take a long time (thousands of earth years) to get that number up there for the eternal population that will inhabit His kingdom. Maybe those who actually did follow Satan would also have a chance to redeem themselves and turn it around as it were.

God loves to redeem the lost. If you mess up and make a wrong choice, don't you like to have another chance? If you find out some fact that you didn't know, don't you correct your thinking accordingly? If all of a sudden you are standing in the presence of the Almighty God but you hadn't really believed He existed (so your life displayed a certain behavior due to that) and then all of a sudden, there you are, would you not want another chance? It will be too late on that day. There will be weeping and grinding of teeth. It is appointed unto man, once to die, and after that, the judgment.

I can't talk you into anything, nor would I want to. If I can talk you into it, then someone can talk you out of it. Human words can't sway you. You have your mind set. But remember, some things were already real before you were born. You can't change certain things. There are laws in this universe that didn't wait for you. I admit you are important, but the world doesn't revolve around you. Don't think too highly of yourself, or the fall will surprise you.

We face an adversary that is cunning and very intelligent. He is a master psychologist and knows the thoughts of man. While he can't take your life, he can offer ideas, situations, and thoughts that seem okay to dwell on that do lead you to destruction. It's an easy and popular path. Many are on it, and many want to get on it and want to stay on it. Sheer numbers won't change the outcome. It didn't change the outcome for the original one-third of angels that followed Satan in his choice. (They might have complained that this isn't fair to put us into this hell area just because we messed up once in heaven.) So God may have put them through the proving ground called earth to see if they will do things differently this time. Time will tell if any of them did anything different. It won't change God's mind to have trustworthy souls forever. He won't be denied His wishes.

I want to know that the trust level is there too and not be worried that the guy over there might hit me when I'm not looking. I don't even want to have them hate me, be jealous, or be anything else but loving. That might be a little selfish of me, but it is also some top-of-the-line peace of mind. How can total peace of mind be present if there is a murderer in our midst? Or if someone is spreading lies and hate? We all see good and evil existing side by side here in this life. They beckon us to choose one or the other. We must choose.

I don't base my choice on just getting out of hell. I have learned to love the innocent, the lovely, and the holy. It is far more attractive and has much more to offer. It is unlimited.

I was so relieved when I found out that Jesus is real. He will make all things balance out for eternity, and He will be our standard. He said, "If I be lifted up, I will draw all men unto me." The problem is we don't lift Him up. Some do with their mouth, but their heart is far from Him. They allow sinful behavior to have a part in their life. Some to a large degree and some just a little bit. Either way, the outcome is the same. Souls are lost due to others behavior.

If you are seriously contending for the faith, don't look at other people's lives for evaluation. Look to Jesus and His life. If you are easily offended by others, then maybe your expectations are not in the right perspective. Look to

Jesus for how to live your life. The church can't seem to quit being religious and fighting over doctrine and money. The souls that seek God wind up disillusioned, hurt, and wounded by the church and those in it.

If you are not contending for the faith but you know you should be, then ask God to create a heart in you that does desire Him. He is faithful, and He will do that for you. King David asked for it, and God did it for him. By the way, God is not a respecter of persons. He will do for you what He has done for others. Just ask. The best is yet to come—happiness, peace, serenity, relationships, warmth, goodness, meaning, direction, contentedness, too many to mention. All good. We are able to imagine it somewhat, but it will be much better than we can perceive.

If you are not contending for the faith and you don't want to contend for the faith and don't care about any of this at all, *please read this next part very carefully*.

If people don't care about others at all, don't care about themselves, don't care about animals, the earth, or any other subject, they truly walk on the most dangerous ground there is. This is all the good there is for you, and it is the best you will see. The worst is yet to come. An eternity of remorse, loneliness, despair, regret, and torment. No one else will be there with you. No one will say, "I told you so," except for you to yourself. No words can describe the anguish felt by the damned soul. Eternal damnation cannot be felt during this life; it can be imagined by us a little bit, and it is so that we don't allow it. Read the rule book. Search the Scriptures. It helps us to avoid it at all costs if we try. We run this race called life. Run according to the rules. Be eligible. Be wise, for your adversary, the devil, seeks those he may devour.

www.ingramcontent.com/pod-product-compliance
Lightning Source LLC
Chambersburg PA
CBHW052116070526
44584CB00017B/2508